All About Dinosaurs

T0101111

Velociraptor

Daniel Nunn

Heinemann
LIBRARY
Chicago, Illinois

© 2015 Heinemann Library
an imprint of Capstone Global Library, LLC
Chicago, Illinois

To contact Capstone Global Library, please call 800-747-4992, or visit our web site www.capstonepub.com

All rights reserved. No part of this publication may be reproduced or transmitted in any form or by any means, electronic or mechanical, including photocopying, recording, taping, or any information storage and retrieval system, without permission in writing from the publisher.

Edited by Daniel Nunn and James Benefield
Designed by Tim Bond
Picture research by Tracy Cummins
Production by Helen McCreath
Originated by Capstone Global Library Ltd

Library of Congress Cataloging-in-Publication Data
Nunn, Daniel, author.

Velociraptor / Daniel Nunn.
pages cm.—(All about dinosaurs)
Summary: "This book takes a very simple look at the Velociraptor dinosaur, examining what it looked like, what it ate, how it behaved, and its special skills and features such as its sharp teeth and claws. The book also discusses how we know about Velociraptor today, showing where fossils are found and how scientists put them together."—Provided by publisher.
Includes bibliographical references and index.
ISBN 978-1-4846-0208-9 (hb)—ISBN 978-1-4846-0215-7 (pb) 1. Velociraptor—Juvenile literature. 2. Dinosaurs—Juvenile literature. I. Title.

QE862.S3N866 2015
567.912—dc23 2013040469

Acknowledgments
We would like to thank the following for permission to reproduce photographs: Alamy p. 21 (© Kayte Deioma/ZUMAPRESS.com); Corbis pp. 17 (©Mark Stevenson / Stocktrek Images), 18 (© Walter Geiersperger); Getty Images pp. 4, 8, 15 (Daniel Eskridge/Stocktrek Images), 11 (Yuriy Priymak/Stocktrek Images), 19 (DANI POZO/AFP), 23 (Ulrich Baumgarten); The Image Works p. 12 (©The Natural History Museum); Science Source pp. 6 (José Antonio Peñas), 20 (John Mitchell); Shutterstock pp. 5a, 9, 10, 13 (Michael Rosskothen), 5b (iSIRIPONG), 5c (defpicture), 5d (Mogens Trolle), 7 left (Ralf Juergen Kraft), 7 right (Chepko Danil Vitalevich), 10 background (design36), 27 (tratong); Superstock pp. 16 (Kevin Eaves), 14 (Stocktrek Images).

Cover photograph of Velociraptor (computer-generated 3D illustration) reproduced with permission of Shutterstock (Michael Rosskothen).

Back cover photograph of Velociraptor reproduced with permission of Shutterstock (Michael Rosskothen).

Every effort has been made to contact copyright holders of material reproduced in this book. Any omissions will be rectified in subsequent printings if notice is given to the publisher.

Printed in the United States 5594

Contents

Meet Velociraptor 4
What Was Velociraptor Like? 6
Where Is Velociraptor Now? 16
Where In the World? 22
Picture Glossary. 23
How to Say It 23
Index 24
Notes for Parents and Teachers . . .24

Meet Velociraptor

Velociraptor was a dinosaur.
Dinosaurs lived long ago.

Dinosaurs were reptiles.
Snakes, crocodiles, and lizards
are reptiles that live today.

What Was Velociraptor Like?

Velociraptor was a small dinosaur.

Velociraptor was as big as a turkey!

Velociraptor may have had feathers.

Velociraptor had a long tail.

Velociraptor ran on two legs.

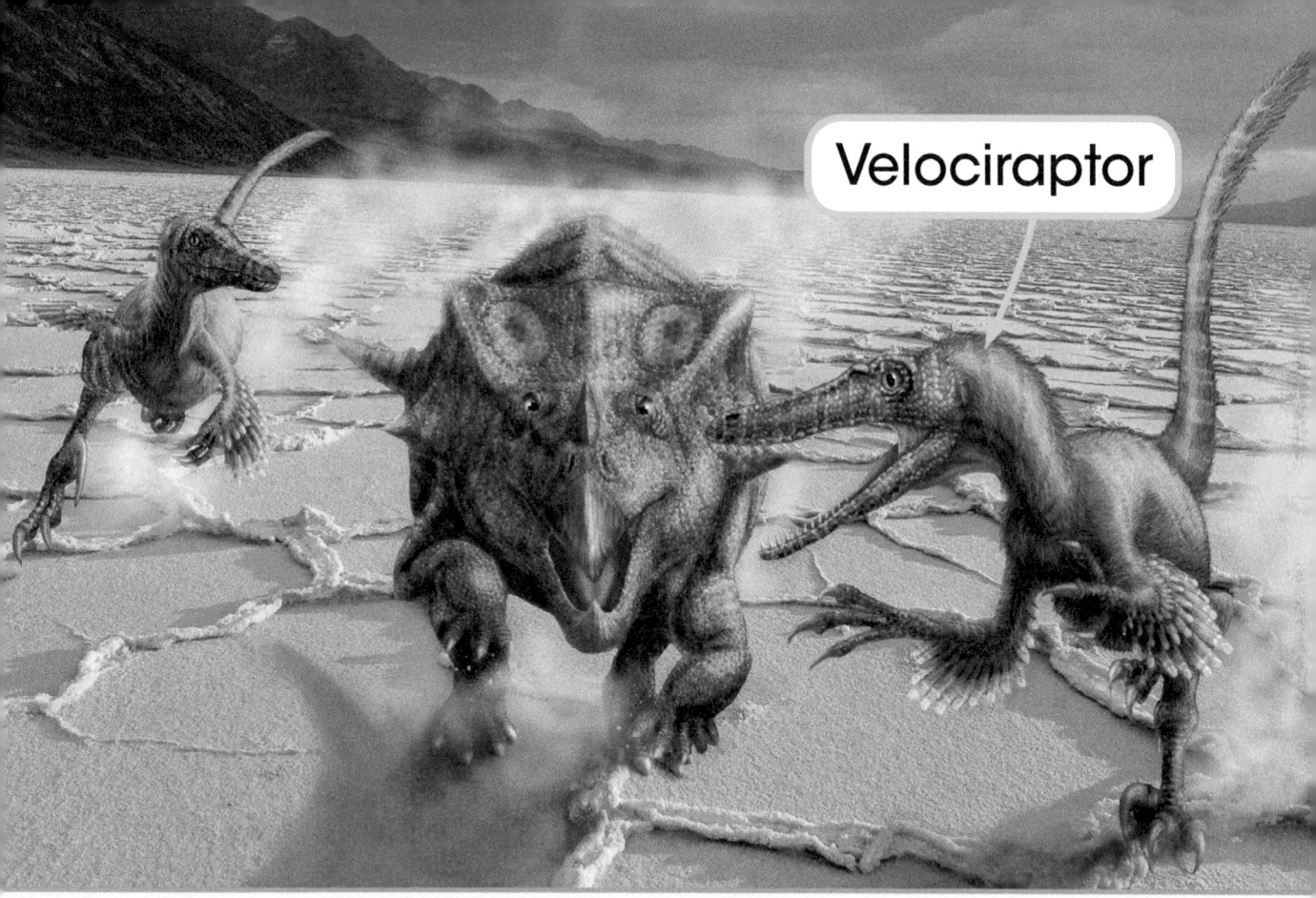

Velociraptor was fast!

Velociraptor had sharp teeth.

Velociraptor had long arms and sharp claws.

Velociraptor used its claws to attack other dinosaurs.

Velociraptor hunted small animals.

Where Is Velociraptor Now?

Velociraptor is extinct. There are no Velociraptors alive now.

All the dinosaurs died long ago.

We learn about dinosaurs from fossils.

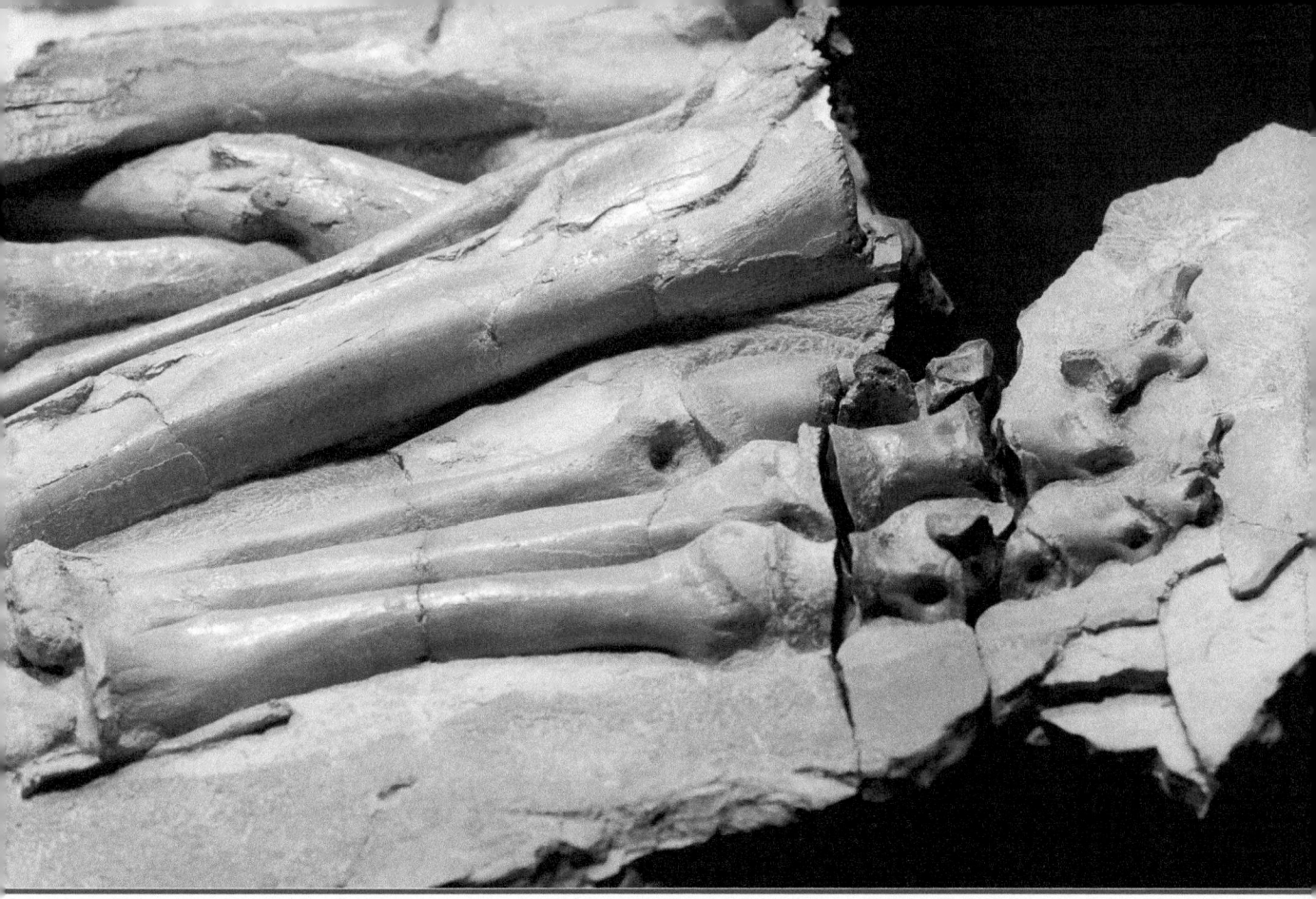

Fossils are animal bones that have turned to rock.

People find fossils in the ground.

Fossils show us what Velociraptor looked like.

Where In the World?

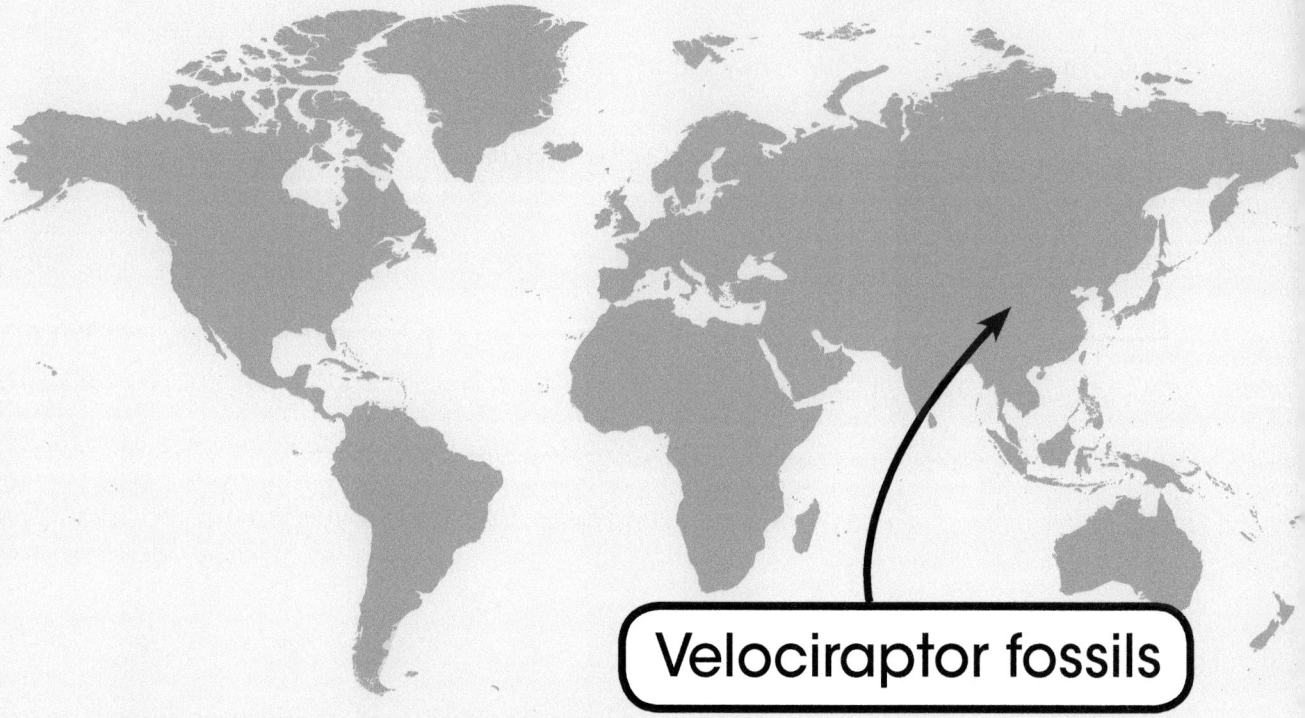

Velociraptor fossils have been found in Mongolia and China.

Picture Glossary

fossil animal bones or parts of a plant that have turned into rock

reptile cold-blooded animal. A lizard is a reptile.

How to Say It

Velociraptor: say "veh-loss-ih-rap-tor"

Index

claws 13, 14
crocodiles 5
feathers 8
fossils 18–21, 22, 23
lizards 5
reptiles 5, 23
snakes 5
teeth 12

Notes for Parents and Teachers

Before Reading
Ask the children to name some dinosaurs. Ask them if dinosaurs are around today. Talk about how some dinosaurs ate plants and others ate other dinosaurs. Can they think of ways these dinosaurs might have been different? Have they heard of Velociraptor? Find out if they already know anything about this dinosaur.

After Reading

- Look at pictures of Velociraptor and compare them to pictures of birds. Can they see anything that looks the same? Talk about the size of Velociraptor, its feathers, and its claws. What are the differences between Velociraptor and birds? Talk about how scientists think birds are descended from dinosaurs.
- Make fossils. Roll out play dough and ask the children to cut out circles with cookie cutters. Then press small plastic toy dinosaurs sideways into the dough. Make a museum for your "fossils."